T0065236

The Spirit of the Father

The Spirit of the Father

by

Randy Brown

THE SPIRIT OF THE FATHER

iUniverse books may be ordered through booksellers or by contacting:

iUniverse
1663 Liberty Drive
Bloomington, IN 47403
www.iuniverse.com
844-349-9409

ISBN: 978-1-6632-2832-1 (sc)
ISBN: 978-1-6632-2835-2 (e)

Print information available on the last page.

iUniverse rev. date: 08/31/2021

Dedication

I dedicate this book to Victor Roy Brown who is my biological father. Victor has been my greatest inspiration and encourager in all of the endeavors that the Lord has placed in my spirit. So I say thank you dad.

Table of Contents

Table of Contents

The Blessing of the Father

Chapter 1

"And the Lord said unto Moses, gather unto me seventy men of tile elders of Israel, whom thou knowest to be elders of tile people, and officers over them; and bring them unto the tabernacle of tile cong regntion, that tliey may stand therewith thee. And I will come down and talk with thee there; and r will take of the spirit which is *upon thee and l will put it on tlrem; and they shall bear the burden of tlie people with thee, thnt thou benr it not thyself alone"* (Numbers 11:16-17).

Moses was accustomed to ministering to these thousands of people by himself. He would sit out in the sun from its rising to its setting: prophesying, counseling, and giving ministry. However, now God was allowing him to release seventy of the elders of Israel into the service and leadership of the people.

> *"And Moses went out, and told the people the words of the Lord, and gathered the sevent-y men of the elders of the people, and set them around the tabernacle. And the Lord came down in the cloud and spake unto him, and he took of the spirit that was upon him and gave it unto the seventy elders; and it came to pass, that, when the spirit rested upon them, they prophesied and did not cease."* Numbers 11:24-25

Now these seventy men had never prophesied before. Up until that point, the only people that had been given the gift of prophecy were Moses, Miriam, and Aaron. However, now all seventy of these men were prophesy ing due to the fact that the spirit of the Lord was passed down through Moses and began to rest upon them.

> *"But there remained hvo of the men in the camp, the name of the one was Eldad, and the name of the other Medad."* Numbers 11:26

These were two of the elders of Israel. Take note that both of them were ... *'dads.* Eldad and Medad had re mained in the camp, yet,

> *"the spirit rested upon them, and ... They prophesied in the camp. And there ran a young nwn, and told Moses, and said, Eldad and Medad do prophesy in the camp."* Numbers 11:27

Three elements of *Moses'* spirit came upon these men: 1) leadership and counseling 2) prophesy ing 3) a fa thering position. The only people to release blessings in Israel were the fathers.

In these days and times, we lack the atmosphere of the fathers across the globe. There are fathers out there. They may have *children,* but they are not fathers. The issue or distinguishing mark of a father is to *release* something unto the children... to give something" unto his seed."

For every father you show me, J will show you a hundred men who are *not* fathers.

The spirit that was upon Moses dropped on these men. They star ted counseling and leading. They started prophesying, and they entered i nto a fatherly realm to release certai n blessings in the midst of the people. We are not ta lking about the spirit of God. We are ta lking about the spirit of God in a man. We are not referring to a man's spirit. There is a spirit of a man -just like there is a spirit of a woman. However, there is a lso a spirit of God in a father role that manifests itself inside of the temple of this individual call ed a man. This spirit enables man to pour out to others. A father w ho does not give is no good! He was created to give, to release, and to bless! Genesis 27:27,41 refers to Isaac blessing

Jaco b and Esau. Genesis 27:41 *"And Esau hated jacob because of the blessing wherewith his father blessed hint ..."* The blessing was meant for Esau because he was the firstborn. When Esau came and begged, Isaac blessed Esau. Yet he told Esa u, "You will serve your brother." He was saying in essence to Esau, you will never be greater than your brother. There is a certa in release that comes only from a father (not from a mother).

Mothers have a great role in the kingdom. You cannot get away from the mothers of Israel, and you need the mothers of Zion. You need the spiritual mothers to pour in to us. However, without a father's presence, even the mother will come up sho rt! You remember the old ri ddle, "What came first - the chicken or the egg?" What was rel eased first, the man or the woman? The man was created first in the Garden of Eden. There are issu es in the father's spiri t, that if they are not released, certain manifestations will *never* ta ke place!

Remember when Joseph brings Manasseh and Ephraim to be blessed by Jacob, he put Ephraim on the l eft side of Jacob. He put Manasseh on the right side. Manasseh was the eld est brother and Ephraim was the younger brother. Joseph said, "Daddy bless them. Release your blessing upon them." The Word states that the eyes of Jacob had become dim, yet in the spirit rea lm, he knew what he was doing. Jacob took his right hand and grabbed a hold of Ephra im on the lef t side. Then he too k his left hand and gra bbed a hold of Manasseh. When you read the scripture, Joseph said, "Daddy, you are making a mistake!" Jacob said, "I am not ma king a mistake." The blessing bel on gs to the second child. That made Joseph jump because he knew the importance of the release of the father's blessing. This cenario illustrates that on the right hand of the f ather, there is power! What transpired through this process is, in actua lity, th at both Ephraim and Manasseh received the spirit of the Father on them through transference from a spiritual father Oacob). They both received transference f rom the Father in and upon their lives.

There could be several reasons why we, as a church body, have difficu l ty receiving spiritual impartation from men in fatherly positions. One reason we have diff iculty receiv ing from men in fatherly positions in the church is because we were not able to receive from our fathers at home. That is one reason. Ano ther reason is that dad dy at home was "a dog." Perhaps daddy was not there at all while we were growing up. Maybe there was an inconsistent presence of a father. You see, when daddy is not there, he cannot give anything. Some times the situation is that the father is living in the house, but he still is not there! Therefore he could not give a ny thing. Then, the children leave their natural realm of the world and come into the house of God and the spiritua l fathe rs of the house try to release something into them. However, because they are used to not receiving from a father, they find it dif fic ult to receive in the church world. Therefore, they need the revelation that certain things only come from a father.

There are powerful women of God across the earth w ho shake nations! My wife knows a woman of God over in East Africa whose congregation is well over 50,000 people every Sunday mornin g! Ye t she still needs a *father* because there are blessings on the right hand of a father. There is *power* and *dominion* on the right hand of a father. If I do not embrace what a father can give, or I still think with the mind I had when I was in the world, I only harm myself. If my mind remains stuck on what my father did, the fac t that my father was never home, or that my father was no good, or that my father raped me, or that he was perverted, then when the fathers in the house of God attempt to release a blessing, I cannot receive. Do not connect the fathers of Egy pt with the fathers of the house of God. We want what they are releasing! We want the anointing of those godly men to come upon *us*.

The Kings of Israel called Elijah "fathe r," not prophet. There is a blessing that comes from a father. When Elijah was taken to hea ven, Elisha called him f ather. The most violent thing one of my children can do is say to me, "Apostle;" I'm leaving to go to school. Apostle bless me." They do not need any apostolic blessing. They need a blessing that comes only from a father. My kids are trained to say to me, "Daddy bless me before I take that test. Bless me bef ore I go back to school. Bless me while I go down here for that job interview." There is a release from a father that cannot come from anyone else!

The Word of God says that Abraham was a prophet? The Word says he was the father of many nations as well. This father had the abili ty to possess lands and territory-release and declare blessings that no one else can declare. God made a statement to Abraham that *"whoever curses you will be cursed and whoever blesses you will be blessed."* When you examine the book of Genesis, it seems as if Genesis keeps repeating itself. It seems as if Isaac went through and did some of the same things as Abraham. Why? Because it was the spirit of the father that was deposited within him *manifesting* itself. Jacob went and did so me of the same things that Isaac did because he carried within him the sa me spirit of his father. The Holy Ghost comes to lead, guide, comfort, and instruct. Even the *Holy Ghost* releases the unction of the spirit of the Father so that it can be deposited into the children.

Psa lm 127:3 *"Lo, child ren are a heritage of the Lord and the fruit of the womb* is *his reward."* Those that were birthed in the spirit, prayed through in the spirit, and were travailed for in the spirit, are the fruit of his re*ward.* Psalm 127:4 *"As arrows are in tile hand of a mighty man; so are children of* *the youth."* They are referring to those that *are* youthful in the spirit. Psalm 127:5 says, *"Happy is the man that ha s his quiver full ...."* The Bible refers to children in the hand of a mighty man or a h a ppy daddy, because the quiver bel ongs to the father. The issue is that the *stronger* the father, the farther he drives his children. Take, for example, a son that is trying to buy a house. This son's father refuses to cosign for his mortgage. The father claims that he is i n enough debt a lready and moreover has to focus on taking care of his ow n household. On the other hand, a father could take the position that, "Son, you better press on and buy that house. After you get that house settled, try to pick up another hou se and take on mul tiple properties and lands." Can you see the second father la unching the son? Do you see that the second father is sending his son into a place of prosperity? The second father went on to say that, "You have a calling to preach. It would be good if you owned about five to ten houses, so that you would not even have to work a natural job any more. You could take care of these houses and when the income from these houses comes in, you could travel the world and preach. When you get the first house, invite me because I want to bless that house." Do you hear the launching? However, a lot of fathers do not do that. They would start the conversation, "when I was..." My response to that is: "I do not want to hear when you was...!" If you were in *bondage* when you "were", then the outcome does not apply to me! I want to hear what you believe I am capable of doing and performing. I want you to lau nch me somewhere deep into the ozone's of the spirit so that I might brea k through in the realms that only *supernatural believers* can break through!The only one that can do that is the father.

When a mother imparts blessing, it is wonderful. There is a n understanding that children have that nurturing comes f rom their mother, so that if they do not do well, Mom will simply und erstand that they did their best. The fact is that people do not like going back and telling their father that they did their best and ca rne up *short!* In the arms of their mother they are going to get loving and nurturing. The father is going to say, "what's wrong with you, why did you not take it? Why didn't you *possess* it?" A father will challenge his clilldren and push them -drive them, stay af ter them, and take them in another direction. That is w hy the l a unching comes from the father. So, your father has the power to kill you or make you live! He can tell you that you are *great* or that you are no good!

I never used the term "apostle" until I was twenty-five years old. Yet I have been preaching since the age of seventeen. One d ay when I reached a bout my midtwenties, I woke up and heard the voice of the Lord say, "Though art an apostle." Did God just *decide* to make me an apostle at age twenty-five? No. The apostolic call was in me from the foundation. For some supernatural reasoning, at age twenty-five, it woke up! I realized what was in me. In the early 1980's, other gifts awakened in me: miracles and hea ling. The problem was, I did not realize it and therefore I did not start operating in it until about 1980 or 1981. Financial breakthroughs started operating in me in the middle to late 1980's. I believe those gifts were there from the *foundation.* The problem is a lot of times that we do not realize what is in our spirit already because we have not yet tapped into its fullness. Perhaps the gifts are still asleep, or have not yet become manifest.

I believe one factor that causes the gifts to awaken within us is the *spirit of the father* because the spirit of the father has quickening power.

To break down the revelation a step further, life is in the blood. The blood flows through the seed, and the seed comes by way of man. So it is not a natural seed, but a spiritual seed released from the father. The purpose is to quicken your spiritual desires from your womb (whether you are male or female) and all of a sudd en you find yourself pulling on your fathers a nointing! The manifestation may have just started happening, but the gift was in you, lying dormant, from the beginning. You just needed somebody to fertilize it and call it out. That is where the father comes in because he can release certain blessings on your behalf and cause you to go higher. Even if something is not in you, if it is in your father, it flows downward and comes to you.

That is why we have to be very careful both *spiritu ally* and *naturally.* If your natural father was a failure, odds are that you are going to be a failure a lso. That is w hat you were raised up to be, to be on ly so successful and then collapse. You have got to then see where the spiritual roots that are feeding you are coming from. Therefore, you can manif est su ccess and become somethin g greater than what you are at this point, whether it wakes up what is in you or causes what is in the spiritua l father to be released onto you. It is through this process that you can become greater than what you are already.

The problem is a lot of times that we do not *want* to receive from the father because we are und er the impression that it belittles us. No one ever wants help. We have a soci ety of people today that wants to be *self-made.*

We want to be able to say, "I did this all by myself. I put myself through college," instead of reali zing that we needed a deposit from a father because it gave u s a jump-start in life! A deposi t from a true spiritual father gives a boost and catapults you into a position maybe five, ten, fifteen, or twenty years farther than where you would have been, just by embracing it and not being offended by it.

There was a church in Africa where every time the Bishop went out, he would have two preachers in his car. One of the leaders in his church said to him, "Just let me drive you and I will sleep in the car." The Bishop responded, "I cannot guarantee I will feed you every day because I am taking care of two other preachers and myself." So they traveled and the driver would go around with the Bishop of this African church to all diff erent locations. And, he would sleep in the car. When the preachers would bathe, they would get the driver a bucket of water and he wo uld go somew here in the building and bathe. Yet the sa me driver insisted on driving the Bishop every whe re. He would even rise ea rly, before anyone else would get up, to iron the Bisho p's clothes and prepare things. People did notrealize that he was *pulling* at his father's spirit. He did this for nearly four to five years and then the Bishop died. When the Bishop d ied, the two preachers took over the church. The church continued going forwa rd, but there was no progression of greatness, unlike the Bishop, who was a l ways breaking d own spiritual ba rriers, and growing l a rger and larger.

One day word came from the other side of the country that a church started a bout eighteen months prior had already grown to be one of the largest churches in the area. It was not from the transplant of church members. People were coming in by the m asses and bein g sa ved in large numbers. In a n eighteen-mo nth peri od, the preacher of this church was preaching to a bout five to seven thousand people. The preachers went to visit the church, wondering: "who is this guy? Where did he come from?" However, when they got there, they were in *shock*, because behind the pulpit stood the Bishop's driver! The reason they did not know who he was is because all they used to call him was "son" and "boy." No one knew his name. One of the Pastors said that the frightening thing was, he talked just like the Bishop. Wh en he walked across the platform, he walked just like the Bishop. He *taught* like the Bishop, and preached like the Bishop, as well. When they reflected back, they said that all he did was drive, but when he preached, there were prophe tic moves of God and miracles taking place, just like the Bishop. All of that laboring that the chauffeur did was due to the fact that he wanted something. He wanted the spirit of the father. That is why Elisha said, "I want twice your spirit." You cannot get your father's spirit if you do not put yourself in a child's positio n to em brace information.

"When I was a child, I spoke as a child..." there is a *season* for your childhood. When you are in the season of your childhood, glean and possess information! You do not get sa ved and then two years later travel the world preaching. It is completely contrary to the Word of God. No one has ever been successful getting saved and then two years later starting to preach. Those that say Paul got saved and then bega n preaching need to read properly. He s pent three years in the Ara bian Deser t, and then he sat under Peter and the other apostles. Though he was the *greatest* of the apostles, he sat under them all so they could father him and give him information. We come up short because we do not wan t input from certain realms, because we think we know something. Then when we come up short, it is because we would not permit so meone to launch us like an arrow into the deep. The only one that can launch you deep and far is your father!

When the sons came for a blessing from both Isaac and Jacob, the sons would kiss their fathers. He would kiss them on their neck and embrace them. You know what that is? Getting personable with their fathers. Being personable does not mean that you have to be with someone everyday, twenty-f our hours a day, seven days a week. It means being able to embrace the personality in such a way that you can take something from it. When Esau ca me to his father, and he didn't come empty-handed. That is how Jacob tricked Esau out of his blessing. Jacob put on animal clothing so he smelled like his bro ther. He made his mother cook the venison so that it smelled like his brother's food and presented the food and said, "Now Daddy, eat." Then his father smelled it and blessed him.

In the Word, it says "call no man Father" (capital f). The Bible only makes one reference to that. There is *only* one Father. The Word is referring to the fact that there is only one God, our Father. Yet Pa ul says that we have many fathers here on earth. That is why Timothy pulled Paul close. If Paul passed the m antle to a nyone in the New Testament, odds are it was Timothy.

He used to share the rhema he received with Timothy. Timothy used to write for him. Timothy u sed to sit and listen to council from him. Timothy used to tra vel with him. So, if anyone got it, the odds are it was Timothy. We need to get close, so we can get *something* because what was spoken from back in eternity is in you! If anyone knows how to unlock it, it is the daddy. The problem is that if we could not receive from the daddy that we grew up with, or we did not have one at all, we are not going to listen to a daddy inside the house of God. The result is that we will come up short!

Another issue is that someone co uld call me a father and be thinking in their spirit, "you dirty dog!" It is not a matter of what title you call someone by, it is an issue of what is going on in your spirit! The revelation is that certain things will not take place unless they are released according to and in-line with the principles of the Word of God. One of these principles is that a father is the only one that has a right to speak certain things and release certain blessings. The unleashing of those gifts in the spiritual rea lm takes you to a new location. The spirit of the father in the midst of your life will make you what God wants you to be. That is why we get *tormented* many times because we look at the heads in the kingdom sometimes the sa me way we look at the folks we dealt with o utside in the world.

The Mercy of the Father

Chapter 2

"The Lord is longsuffering, and of great mercy, forgiving iniquity and transgression, and by no means clearing the guilty, visiting the iniquities of the fathers upon the children unto the third and the fourth generation. Pardon, I beseech thee, the iniquity of this people according unto the greatness of thy mercy, and as thou has forgiven this people, from Egypt even until now" (Numbers 14:18-19).

We serve a merciful God. It is the mercy of God that has rescued us until this time to bring u s to this location of life. And, it is the mercy of God that has brought u s safely through all of the transitions and the dispensations of the world. I remember in the Word of God, it states that God said, "I repent of this thing called man that I have created." God wanted to do away with us. There are at least three to six occasions in the writings of the "Laws of Moses" where God was going to destroy Israel. He said, "I am fed up with these people and their murmuring, complaining, and cursing at me." God told Moses, "I am going to kill all of them!" Moses and Aaron threw themsel ves down and said, "God, give them another chance. Give them another chance. Give them a break." So the God that we serve is merciful!

Sometime we do not realize the degree of mercy of God. That is why sometimes in the kingdom of God, some of us Christians become frustrated because we see another Christian acting unjustly and we stand back wa iting for the lightning bolts of heaven to strike. When we see someone doing illegal things here on earth or we see ungodly realms being operated in, we start to wonder "why hasn't God dea lt with that person?" You know what? You do not want God to dea l with anybody. I know you are glad, as r am that we are in the dispensation of jesus Christ where love and mercy do a bound. Withou t that love and mercy of God, we would *all* be in big trouble. We would all be extremely messed-up and headed in the wrong direction. There is a need for the mercy of the Lord!

I read a passage and it was shocking to me! I had rea d this passage before, but this time it somehow jolted me! Numbers 15:32-34 states,

> *"and while the children of Israel were in the wilderness, they found a man t/ wt gathered sticks on the Sabbath day. And they that found hill gathering sticks brought him unto Moses and Aaron, and unto all the congregation. And they*

put him in a ward, because it was not declared what should be done to him".

They did not know what to do with him. This guy was picking up sticks on church day, o n the day of worship.

> *"And the Lord said unto Moses, 'The man shall surely be put to death; all the congregation shall stone him with stones without the camp. And all the congregation brought him without the camp, and stoned him with stones, and he died as the Lord commanded Moses."* Nu mbers 15:35-36

He died for picking up sticks on the Sabbath. They killed the man! I thought that was amazing! It sho ws you how under the Old Testament, God left no space for mistakes. The theme of the Old Testament was, "Do it right or do not do anything at all." Isn't it wonderfu l how we live under the grace of Jesus Christ? Some of u s have made enough mistakes that we would have been stoned five or six times alrea dy. In fact, you would be in your house never coming out for the cuts and bruises upon your body from the stonings. There is mercy in the Word of God that seemed to be released from the Father, but it had to be pulled upon in the Old Testament. Yet in the New Testament, because of Christ, there is mercy!

The Bible says in John 8, the Pharisees caught a woman in the very act of adultery. That mea ns she was involved in sex ua l intercourse when someone walked in and caught her. The issue here is that you cannot be invol ved in a sex ual encounter unless you have co mpany. l strongly believe that the reason they did not indict the man is because he was a Pharisee. I believe that the man was a preacher and they did no t want their" preacher f riend" to be ca ught in the midst of this mess. That is the only excuse that I can come up with. This man had to be a person of power and position! Meanwhil e, they brought this woman to Jesus said that she ha d been ca ught in the very act of adultery and that according to the "La w of Moses," she had to be stoned. These folks loved stoning people! When the men brought forth their accusation, aski ng Jesus for *his* opi ni on, He began to write with his finger in the dirt. Perhaps He was writing down other sins, because he stood up and said, *"He that* is *without sin, cnst the first stone."* Since we have all been born into a world of sin, we need mercy!

The people that carne and accused her, the Bible says, drop ped the stones and dispersed, and Jes us sai d, *"Where are thine accusers?" She said, "Lord, 1 do not know." He said, "I do not accuse you either. Go thy ·way and sin no more."* In other words, from this point on, live a godly and holy life. Romans 9:15 states, *"I will have mercy upon whom I will have mercy, and I will have compassion on whom I will have compa ssion."* He wants to have mercy on us.

I believe that so me people take advantage of the mercy of God and of the grace of God. I believe that some people try to push God to see what they can get away with. Yet our God is still a mercif ul God. The issue is that we try to ta ke advantage of his mercy. It is like the child that keeps being disrespectfu l and rude to his or her father or mother. I sat in the dentist's office with my kids one-day and a mother said to her daughter, "Listen now, when they extract this too th, it won't hurt." The child said, "Ma, shut up, I am fine!" This was a si xteen or seventeen year old child. The father was sitting there reading and the mother said, "Afterwa rds, we will go by your aunt's house and order a pizza and you can rent a movie." The child responded, "Did I ask you for pizza?" This conversation went on for a while. By the time she responded to her mother the fourth time, out of nowhere came the hand of judgment! Her father slapped her and the imprint of his hand was on her thigh. She did not even scream. That is how we sometimes act with God. We try to keep taking advantage because we figure there is mercy. I tell you that judgment day is coming. The day of the Lord's reckoning is coming. So I do not want to take advantage of his mercy.

The Bible says that He is a compassionate and mercif ul God. 2 Corinthians 4:1 says that, *"Therefore since we have this ministry, as we have received mercy, we faint not."* 2 Corinthians 4:16, *"For which cause we faint not; though our outward man perish, yet the inward man is renewed day by day."* Do you know why you are renewed day-by-day? It is simply because of the mercy of God. The mercy of God makes you feel new every morning. You realize that if it were not for *his* mercy, you wou ld not be where you are right now. The house, the job, the family, the situation, the circumstances, the cluldren, no matter what condition everything is in -if it was not for His mercy...where would we be? His mercy endureth forever! Our God is a merciful God, our God is a compassionate God, and our God is a lov ing God. For example, in Matthew 15:21-28 when the woman comes to Jes us and says, "Lord, my da ughter is ill," and Jesus says, "I will not give my children's bread to a dog." She states, "Yes, Lord, you're right. But even the dogs eat the crumbs from the table. "J esus says, 'You've got good f aith, woman. Go thy way; your child is heal ed'". He is truly a merciful God. He did not want to turn a ny body a way. He was trying to reach Israel f irst. He shows mercy toward s us f or the errors that we ma ke to pull us to a place that we can operate in the blessings of God.

I Timothy 1:13 says, *"Who was before a blasphemer and a persecutor, and injurious; but I obtained mercy, because I did it ignorantly in unbelief"* You know when you get mercy? When you do things, just because you are stupid. That is when you get mercy. When *I* intentionally plot to disturb my brother, there is no mercy. God just does not know what to do with me because I am washed in the blood.

Some of you might have grown up as an *only* child, but when you come out of a house with several children, there is always one child acting up. It seems like when there are five and six kid s, one a l ways seems to have the d evil in them. Every body else seems to flow together and get into a rhy thm and one just cannot seem to do right and rubs against every body. He basically rubs aga inst the gra in. He causes diff ic ult circumstances and situations to occ ur all the time inside the fa mily setting. It is the sa me tlung in the kingdom of God. There is always somebody acting up in the kingdom of God. There is always somebody causing trouble in the kingdom of God. There is a l ways somebody whose brain is not working in the kingdom of God. In the church, among the cruldren of God, in the fa mily of God, in the body of Christ universal, do you know what ma intains the abili ty for us all to stay together? It is the mercy of God. This is what happens in the world a l ot of times. We grow up and all of a sudden, we disassociate ourselves from that sister that used to rub us the wrong way. At times, we cause ourselves not to interact with that brother. We no longer wa nt to talk to that one anymore because we could not seem to get a long in the past. The fact rema ins, however, is that there is always mercy. When you are in the family of God, you cannot just disassociate, because no matter how hard you try, we both have the blood of Jesus on our l ives and we have received mercy.

This is why when you read in the Word of God, that they ca me to Jesus and asked Him, "Lord, how many times do I have to forgive trus guy a nyway?" Jesus said, "Seven timesseventy" (or four hundred and ninety times). You have to forgive four hundred and ninety times a day. This is what the blood does. The blood causes us to ta ke on a position of mercy that allows us to look beyond the fa ults of another and realize that may be what they did was in ignorance. I can point to times when Paul, the apostle, says, "Be not i gnorant." Do you know why he was addressing that? It was not just f or spiritual reasons, but because some folks need help! They intentionally want to vex you, to trouble you, to bother you, and to get under your skin. The problem is that you, as the mature believer, should be able to stand. You, as the mature believer, should be able to show mercy. Though they did something that they should not have done, though they did so mething that they should not have even tried to do, there is mercy. Though they should not have ma de maneuvers on your husband in the church, there is mercy. Though they should not have ta ken the tithe money out of the en velopes in the back room w hile they were co unting it and put it in their pocket, there is mercy.

I was in a preacher's office after a crusade one day and the preacher said, "That meeting was so powerful, we've go t to have you back. Let's cel ebrate!" I figured we were going to lunch or somethin g, and he pulls out of the desk drawer a bottle of gin. You know what I attribute that to? They are ignorant! If there were no mercy, we would be lost. lf there were no mercy, we would be in tro uble. If we were not being mercif ul, the sa me God that told them, "stone this man for pi cking up sticks," he would be likely to kill somebody for touching your wife. He would probably kill somebody for stealing your job. You know he would kill somebody for cursing and swearing in all likelihood, he would kill somebody for using drugs as well. Yet because of his mercy, we are still a live. The Word of God says that Jesus makes intercessi on before the Father d ay and night. You see, in the Old Testa ment, they had the mercy seat. They had the a rk, and upon the ark, was the mercy seat. The priest would put bl ood upon the mercy seat so that he could enter into the presence of God. Jesus is our mercy seat. He is before God making petitions, "Father, forgive them ..." Do you remember when Steven said, "Jesus, forgive themthey do not know what they are doing." The Bible says, people stripped him and stoned him. Yet he turned around and said, "Father, hold not this sin to their charge. Father, they don't know what they are doing." You have to be joking!

The Word says that the young men need to listen to the older men or their fathers in the kingdom. It wi ll save you from meeting the woman in the corridors by night where she takes your sou l to hell. This is what the Word says. Some Christians are in ignorance because they did not want to listen to any information or truth. The problem is that though they have passed through the blood, there is still a stench of sin because they refuse to be enlightened. This is now where the mercy comes in. There are two types of fools in the Bible. That is why when the Bible says, "call no man a fool," it is not just ta lking about someone who is just stupid. It is add ressing the fact that when someone is in a handicapped position, do not mock the person. Some people cannot help themsel ves. When people cannot help themselves, we need to get to a place where we rea li ze that there is mercy for those that know to do better but because of their hand icap cannot.

As a n upstanding Christian, you expect all believers to: behave as you do, to ta l k in tongues like you, to pray li ke you, to worship like you, to jump around and dance like you, to celebrate Jesus like you, and to give their tithes and offerings faithfully, like you. The unfortunate reality is that they cannot function like you because of ignorance. Now you become offended when they interact with you because you say to yourself, "I thou ght they were blood-washed and they knew better." They do not know any better. They cannot do any better. They do not want to do any better. Therefore, the weight of the whole relationship falls on you! You must function. U you say, "Apostle, listen, I do not *have* to take this." Guess what? You have to take it! Do you know why you *have* to take it? You have to take it because Jesus took it. The Word of God says that he was led as a lamb to the slaughter. Father, forgive them. They do not know what they are doing. When people in the kingdom do things that are out of line and irrational, do not come and make an appointment in the office. Forget the appointment. Don't tell anybody what they did. Show them mercy!

There is an intercession going on before the throne of God day and night. Do you remember the example in Genesis, when Ham saw the nakedness of his f ather, Noah?The Word of God says that his two brothers came in backwards and *covered* their father's na kedness. It sta tes that when their father f ound out that Ham had seen him, Noah cursed his son because Ham was mocking his father and making jest. Some people just do not know any better. The blessing is that there is a Lord Jesus between us and God making petitions, so that mercy is released!

The Word of God says, "to whom you hold sin unto, sin is held unto them. But to whom you free from their sin, they are free from their sin." That mea ns that if a brother does something wrong to me and every time I see him I cannot interact with him because I remember when that brother backed into my car, I need to forgive him. The fact remains that when he backed into the car, he said, "Sorry. We'll ta ke care of it." However, it has been two years and my car still is not ta ken care of. Yet if I hold it against him, the sin remains between us. Let me tell you that condemnation from man can be just as destructive as condemnation from the devil. Where there is mercy, I cannot impute sin to a man. Somebody must stand up and be stronger.

Do you remember that they threw Joseph into a pit and sold *him* as a slave? Do you recall that he went to Potiphar's ho u se and was arrested and throw n into prison again? He was in jail and in bondage longer than he was a live! Years later, when his brothers showed up in Egy pt, some of us would have killed them. When you read the scripture, it says *his* brothers panicked when he revealed himself. They thought he wanted payback. Joseph illu strated, however, that it was not a bout payback, but it is a bout mercy. Joseph made a deci ion that he wou ld no t l owe r himself. There is a need f or us to arise and go higher. Someone needs to make a decision that they do not want to act like the other person because they were foolish and silly. Somebody must hold themsel ves up in stature and say that we are still going to have a conversation. "How are you today?" "Praise the Lord, I'm praying for you today." "How are your parents?" Someone must be mature. In the kingdom of God, we like to make the statemen t: "I am tired of this." You are not tired of anything! Most poeple do not know what it is to really go through something.

Sometimes when people tell me what they are "going through" I just have to la u gh. One man, when we were in Texas, ca me and told Pastor Gayle what he was "going through," and I sta rted la u ghing. He said, "What are you la ughing at?" I said, "That is nothing." He said, "Listen, my life was torn up!" I started laughin g more. I said, "you are with your wife. You are ma rried. You have your own house. You are not going through any thing!" I told him that I co uld show him five people that make what he is going through look like a walk in the park. Now what we must do is to push beyond it. There is a need to rise up beyond our obstacles and stop trying to make an excuse for why we treat our brethren a certain way. There are various realms of mercy. Certa in mercy is only rel eased from God. Yet there is another realm of mercy released from you and me. You mu st be a releaser of mercy! The Bible said when Lazarus ca me out of the grave, Jesus stated, "loose him and let him go!" We need to loose our brethren.

Instead of interacting wrongly with one another, within the kingdom, we need to realize that there is an intercessor -His name is Jesus. We should be releasers so that we do not have to put unnecessary pressure upon people. Take for exa mple the story of Joseph. It teaches u s that we need no t to try to judge and damn somebody just because they were ignorant. There are some blood-washed, born-again, to ngue-ta l king ignorant people.

Hebrews chapter eight refers to the fact that the strength of God and the greatness of God in you are dependent on how much you are able to endure! Does no t the Word of God say that if there is anyone you will not forgive, God will not forgive you either? God is calling us to rea lms of greatness, insight and comprehension, but we do not want to comprehend the mercy of God. Let us reflect upon the fact that Lazarus laid at the rich man's gate. Dog's licked his sores and he ate the crumbs from the rich man's table and he d ied a beggar. He went into the boom of Abraham. The ri ch man died after having a great life and he popped up in hell. He looked over from hell and sa w Abraha iTI and La zar us and said, "Can you hel p me?" What was their res po nse? Basically, i f you read the scriptu res, they say that we woul d like to, but it is not possible. There was a gorge that se pa rated them. Lazarus was not mad at the ric h man. I am sure he wished that he co uld have show n mercy to him. There is a need to show mercy!

Show mercy to you r brother. Show mercy to your sister! I am sorry that they did what they did. I am sorry that your cousin did what he did. I am sorry that your nephew did what he did. I am sorry your friend did what he did. I am sorry that your co-worker and that tongue-talking person, and even the preacher did what he did. I am sorry. Who knows? I could have offended someone the other day when I was traveling. Ia m sorry, but someone must rise hi gher and demonstrate mercy. The *only* way to bring peace is to show mercy! Mercy is in my hands and I shall release i t in Jesus' name. Somebody is suff ering and you have the a bili ty to rescue them. Save them, strengthen them, lead them, and gui de them.

Hebrews 8:12 *"For I will be merciful to their u n righteousness and thei r sin and their iniquity will l remember no more."* You say to yoursell that is the Lo rd, all right.

He is merciful to people's unrighteousness. That is true. They called us Christia ns at Antioch. We are supposed to be just like Him. So guess what? I do not remember your mistake anymore. You know how some people fellowship? You remember the statement that some people used to use "bury the ax" or 'bury the hatchet"? They would bury it, but they would always leave the handle stick ing out of the gro und. Then, as soon as you ma ke a mistake, they w ould say, "I remember when ..." I have been around folks who say, "I don't mea n to star t something, but I just think that we need to address it again..." Release them! Release them!Some poeple are going to be messed up most of their lives. I am sorry! I wish everybody could walk on water. I really do! I w ish every body co uld open the eyes of the blind and ra ise the dead. I wish everybody could pray for two or three hours without taking a breath. I wish every body that became born aga in would stop d rinking, doing drugs, and smoking cigarettes that sa me day.

I w ish they all did. Some people do not. Some come into the church and they do not know any better. They are watching you to follow your example and your lifestyle. The problem is when you react to them wrongl y; all it does is make them revert farther back. I cannot help that they may have acted nasty towards you, but you can at least release some mercy. Release them. Forgive them. Do not impute it to them. Do not hold it over their head. If God in heaven has forgiven you, how much more should you forgive somebody else? Sons remain angry with their daddies for generations of time. Daddies stay mad at their sons for generations of time. Girls stay mad at their mothers for generations of time. Mothers remain mad at daughters. Husbands and wives continue to be mad at each other f or generations. You cannot stay angry! Do you know what anger does to you? It causes your stomach to knot up. You could feel good all d ay, yet when you see that person that you did not release mercy on, you get gripped just like that! Indigestion starts. Heartburn sta rts. Tell somebody there is no justification for being angry and f or not releasing mercy. Just free them!

Do you know whom you are really freeing when you free them? You f ree yourself! That is w hy Ido not hold anything against anybody. My wife will tell you that when we travel, I greet preachers that have treated me like a dog. I ta lk to them, I bless them, I thank God for them, I worship with them, and I might even send them a seed. I love them in Jesus' name. You have to release them. Do not hold onto anything because you are the only one that is going to be af fected. God is try ing to do something great in you!

Your miracle has not come or what you are waiting for has not shown up yet because you are still ho;ding the a x over somebod y's head. You are trying to say it is justifiable because you are a Christian and the reason you cannot get there is, "because if they would just...."

You have to release yourself. Your miracle might be held up just because you are still frustrated. Unfortunately, some things will never be straightened out. Did you ever try to discuss something a month af ter the incid ent? "No, it was cold outside. No, it was hot and rainy." Release it. Simply say, "I am not upset. I am not troubled." Done. There might be a little wound. I might feel a little sore, but you know what? Mercy! Mercy! Mercy! If you do not rel ease that mercy that was released on you first, you are going to find yourself in trouble!

My Father, My Father

Chapter 3

Let's examine the episode when Elijah was taken up in the chariot of fire into heaven. The Word of God says in 2 Kings 2:12:

> *"And Elijah saw it, and he cried, My father, my father, the chariot of Israel, and the horsemen thereof And he saw him no more; and he took hold of I!is own clot/Les, and rent them in hvo pieces."*

Elisha cried out for his father. Elisha is referring to Elijah in this passage as his Father. We as believers need to realize that there is a need for us to acknowledge and embrace the spirit of the Father. Even in dealing with church leadership, there is a relationship beyond that of the apostolic and the prophetic whereby the Lord is allowing people to minister into the lives of individuals who are able to embrace a fatherly ministry. Clearly, direction and instruction from a spiritual father is not always easy to receive. If someone has had difficulties with male figures ou tside the church and a male leader tries to speak to them as a daddy or as a father, the message can be especially difficult to receive. Sometimes walls go up and people start to get offended. When that happens, we may miss out on certain blessings that might have propelled us to reach certain levels or realms of success in our life.

In 2 Kings 6:21 it states, *"And the king of israel said unto Elisha, when he saw them, My father, shall I smite them? Shall I smite them?"* Now, he did not call him Prophet Elisha. He called him father. There was evidently a bond between them. He needed information and instruction from this man. 2 Kings 13:14:

> *"now Elisha was fallen sick ofhis sickness whereof he died. And Joash the King of I srael came down unto him, and wept over hi s face, and said, Oh my fntller, my father, the chariot of israel nnd the horsemen thereof"*

That sounds like when Elijah left. The point is that there was an importance in the connection and relationship not prophetically but from the voice of the father.

The Old Testament prophets did not have to say "thu s saith the Lord," before pouring out of their spirit. A father had the right to make a commandment, a declaration, or a decree. As they spoke in this manner, there was a need to take it not offensively or be bothered by it, but to realize that God is say ing something. When you do some reading on Sa mson, he told his father to go dow n to Gaza and get him one of the bea utiful Philistine women. He always wanted one of the unclean women of the world. He a lways wanted a woman that was not one of Gods choice. His father said, "No, do not go over there!" But Samson would not listen to his father. Samson wou ld not be satisfied with the blessings that were within the House of God. He refused to take the information that was released from the father. Perhaps there could have been si tuations avoided if he had just listened. Sometimes in the kingdom of God, when we reach certain realms of anointing, we do not want counci l or instruction. The issue is that there are principles in the kingdom of God whereby if we could *only* embrace them by absorbing things from our spiritual fathers, God would propel us to higher and deeper levels of anointing.

We entered into a disc u ssion in Guyana while traveling, and the discussion began by talking abou t the fact that everybody has to answer to somebody. The problem in the kingdom is that we do not want to answer to anyone. I do not have to give account to anybody because God is lea ding a n d guiding me." However, that is completely contradicting the Word of God! God always had the disciples a nswer to jesus. Paul, in the beginning still had accountability because the apostles had set up an apostolic board. Everybody had to answer to the board to make sure that the ministry ran well. When you get into the mind set that you do not give account to anyone then you violate the scripture, "Iron sha r pens iron." You break the scripture that states, "Deep calls to deep." You break the scripture where it says, "In the multitude of council, there is wisdom." So we have to be able to listen to authorities and as the bible says, "those who have rule over us," so that we can get information and be restored, be built up, and become esta blished in the name of Jesus. There is a need to embrace, or to gra b hold of certain rea lms of this "spirit of the father" a nointing that releases certa in elements of breakthrough and insights into our lives.

> *"I write not these things to shame you, but as my beloved sons I warn you. For though ye have ten thou sand instructors in Christ, yet have ye not many fathers; for in Christ jesus I have begotten you through the gospel. Wherefore I beseech you, be ye followers of me."* 1 Corinthians 4:14

It is great to have many instructors, but you do not have many fathers. Fathers make themsel ves ava ilable. Instr uctors wan t to come and instruct you, teach you, and leave town. Men that have the spirit of the Father on them will sit there and ta l k with you a little bit. Do you remember in the Word of God when God took the spirit of M oses and d ropped it on seventy other men? All of a sudden, seven ty men who never prophesied and never counseled suddenly f ound that they were prophesy in g and lea ding the peo ple because God took the spirit that was in Moses and put it upon them!

That reminds me of the relationship between Elisha and Elijah. He did not say I want a double portion of the Holy Spirit. He said that I wa nt twice of your spirit. It was the spirit of the man that he wanted. It was the spirit of his father that he wa nted. We need to embrace that realm of anointing and rea li ze that there is something that God wa nts to deposit in us. Paul said you have a lot of instructors, but only a few daddies. One thing a daddy does is give time. I could talk about a lot of things a daddy shou ld do and what children should do, but one thing a father will do is give time.

Somebody came into my off ice tod ay and my da ughter was sitting o n my lap. So they started laughing. "Can't she wait until she gets home? I said, "No, she can't wa it until she gets home." That is my daughter and s he can get my attention a ny time she wants. When we embrace people in a fatherly rea lm, we realize that they serve a certain role -making themsel ves available to be a blessing. Then these spiritua l fathers should ava il wisdom to us and we shou l d bring ourselves to a place in order that we can receive it. It is not just for being patted on the head to say, "You are wond erful." There could be corrections coming. That is normally when these relationships fall a part. Nobody likes being corrected. Yet we all need spiritual; fathers!

I myself drove a visiting Bishop to his hotel roo m on his last night in town. I said to him, "I am taking you back to the hotel because I am getting the blessing." I was ex pecting a spiritual deposit in a fatherly rea lm due to the f act that this was an elderly Bishop. We were di cussing a particular spiritual view. I got up in that hotel room and the Bishop said, "Let me share a revelation with you." I told him that I had a different view on a partic ular matter prior to the discussion. The Bishop, af ter counsel said, "As of today, never think like that again! This is how I want you to think on the matter from now on." Then he pointed out scripture and said, "this is what the Word of God says." The man has preached to thousands in his church and hundreds of churches around the globe. He made a statement and backed it up with scripture. Guess what? The conversation is over. I have always believed that statemen t he made from that night forward.

> *"When Abram was ninety-nine years old, tile Lord appeared unto him and said unto him, 'I am the Almighty God; walk before me, and be thou perfect. And I will make my covenant between me and thee, and will multiply thee exceedingly.' And Abram fell on his face; and God talked with him, saying, 'As for me, behold, my covenant is ·with thee, and thou shalt be a father of many nations."'* Genesis 17:1-4

Interestingly, Abram was a "prophet" as early as Genesis. He is also referred to as a prophet in other parts of the Bible. The Word states that Abraham was a prince with God and a prince with men. The Bible says Abraham was a friend of God. God told Abraham that he would be a father of many nations -not a prophet over the nations. To Jeremiah he said, *"Thou would be a prophet to the nations."* God told Abraham that, *"A father's anointing shall be upon you."* Interestingly, kings apologized to Abraham. Twice when they took his wife, they apologized. Why would a king apol ogize to any man with armies all around him? Because the spirit of a father rested upon Abraham.

Both the Word of God and many cultures of the world, place importance on respecting fathers. In this country we often show disrespect to our elders. Often I come across a mentality of, "I do not have to, or I do not need to respect my elders." In some cultures of the world, daddy can be a "dog," yet when he walks in, "daddy's home" and everybody gets up. They clea n up, straighten the house, and get dinner on immediately. They all ask, "How are you doing, daddy?" They em brace him because they realize that there is a need to acknowledge this man. He can impact their life and set it on a certain course. God calls Abra ham a father of many nations. Genesis 17:5 says, *"Neither shall thy name be called any more Abram, but thy name shall be Abraham; for a father of many nations have I made thee."* Another reason God changed his name is that Abram means, "a man among men", but Abraham means, "father of many nations." His entire identity changed. When God changed Sarah's name, he changed it from Sarai to Sarah-"Sarai" meaning, "one of the princesses", Sarah mea ning, "the princess."

> *"Behold, I will send you Elijah the prophet before the coming of the great and dreadful day of the Lord; And he shall turn the heart of the fathers to their children, and the heart of the children to their fathers lest I come and smite the earth with a curse."* Malachi 4:5

It is interesting that God does not say, "I am going to turn the heart of the children to their parents or the heart of the parents to the children." Momma is a lways aro und, yet the father is the focus. This propheti c a nointing will prompt the men to embrace their chi ldren and the children to embrace their fathers.

A real father does not break the spirit of IUs children. He tries to make them better than even himself. Isaac w as greater than his father Abraham. Jacob greater than his father Isaac; and Joseph greater than his father, Jacob or Israel. Every generation became la rger than the last. These prophetic relationships are intended to help bring a unity to not only natura l families, but spiritual families as well. They help esta blish the Kingdom of God and help build relationships in our every day lives. People have greater understanding, and relationships improve because of a fatherly anointing.

I recently traveled overseas with some pastors. In this particular culture, when a father enters the house, all of the women and children are supposed to meet him and kneel. Nobody moves until given permission. Of course, I did no t like anybody kneeling around me. I believe that one should only kneel before God. One of the other pastors wondered w hy the household knelt when I walked *in.* They apparently believed that I had more to offer than just preaching. They wanted to glean something. Sometimes when they wo uld come, *I* would tell them that they were great in the kingdom, and they would feel uplifted by the time they left. A father is supposed to be a n encourager and a strengthener, not a spirit breaker. A father should never ma ke the statement, "I expected more from you by now," or "I am disappointed in you." When a father makes a gesture or a statement of disappointment, it is alm ost like a slap in the face! In the Jewish religion, when the father cuts a child off, he is cut off for good. The father has the power to ra ise up or destroy his children.

Many times when we come into the kingdom and take this fatherly position, we are greeted by people who have been wounded in one way or another by fathers or other male figures. Therefore, when they come into the Kingdom of God and there is someone w ho is able to take them and edify them, they often pull back. These individuals have to get into a spiritu a l fra me of mind and understand that we in the kingdom are und er the blood. They must believe that the fathers of the House of God are different because they are blood-washed individua ls. What they have to offer is something blessed, and it is going to change them and make them greater in J esus' name.

Proverbs 1:8 *"My son, hear the i nstruction of thy father and forsake not tire law of thy mother"* The father brings a sense of fea r in a situation. The father brings instruction, but the mother brings the law. The law is the Word of God. Proverbs 1:9 *"For they shall be an ornmnent of grace unto thy head, and chains about thy neck."* The father and mother have ba la nce one another. The father brings judgment. Proverbs 3:12 *"For whom the Lord loveth he correcteth;; even as a father the son in whom he delighteth."* A rea l father already sees the destru ction two miles down the road. Maybe he has walked that road, so he makes a preemptive correction. I have four little children. I tell them, "You have no right to have friction among yourselves, because you all have my blood. You must function und er this blood as a unit. One day you are going to need one another's help to come out of a situation, so do not act up now." Then the commandment comes forth, "Apologize!" Even if they did nothing wrong, I want them to apologize. I want them to realize that they can surrender, get right, and love one another.

Proverbs 4:2 *"For I give you good doctrine, forsake ye not my Law."* Most men to drive the following ideas into their sons: strength, masculinity, and the ability to stand up under pressure. I push my son to be a man so that at age forty, he is not living in my house. If I do not drive him to be something, our society will leave *him* undisciplined. The reason there is a weakness in our male society is because there are no strong men in the kingdom to instruct them!*This* is why God was so pleased with David. David tau ght the men strength in several areas: how to cover one another's back, to take care of their women, how to watch out for their city, and how to make sure everything ran and functioned well.

When Deborah was running Israet the Bible says that she was the sole prophet, ruler, and judge. This was a powerful woman! One day, as the Israelites went into battle, the Holy Ghost came upon her. She said, "Barak; it's your time. It's your time. You're going to be the next in command." She was getting ready to tUin over leadership. She said, "You are going to go out and destroy this army." He said, "Well I will go if you come." Anyone who had sense knew that women never went to war. She said, "Fine, I will come, but the victory will be given into the hands of a woman." Who got the victory? A woman, because he was not in his position. God is trying to make us come forward in strength and in a fatherly position. When we fail to do so, then everybody suffers, because we did not take the roles that had been designated to us.

Proverbs 6:20 *"My son, keep thy father's commandment, and forsake not the law of thy mother."* While the mother may say, "flee the very appearance of evil." The commandment of the father may be, "I told you do not bring that girl in this house when I am not home" They both give the law, but the father gives it in the form of a commandment. "Bind the commandments of the law upon your heart, hang them around you r neck." My f ather used to have me shake peoples' hands. If I gra bbed his hand sof tly, he would say, "What kind of wet fish are you giving me to hold onto? Here! Grab my hand like you are holding onto a steering wheel." Then I would gra b his hand firmly, and he would squeeze it back forcefully saying, "Now that is how you grab a man's hand." I am going to tell you something. In my journeys around the world, often it was my handsha ke that determined whether or not I was received. I shook a man's hand one day, and he asked, "Excu se me, sir, who are you?" I said, "I am Apostle Brown fro m the United States." He then gave me a preferentia l seat away from the crowd. I believe it was the handshake. It wasn't soft. I held onto his hand and shook it in a way that a man wants his hand to be shaken. I have benefited because I received my father's commandment.

A spirit is released from the father to help establish the boundaries of the house. It serves to orga nize, strengthen, l ead, and guide, and send us in the right direction.

> *"For the commandment* is *a lamp; and the law is light; and reproofs of instruction are tile way of li fe; to keep thee from the evil woman, from the flattery of the tongue of a strange woman."*
> Proverbs 6:23-24

Here is a commandment that I gave to my da ughter coming home in the car the other night. She said, "Daddy, something happened to me at school today. When I asked what it was she said, "Well, a teacher asked what religion I was." The class was discussing cults and her teacher said, in essence, that it did not matter what religion a person is. We are all the same and we all love God. My da ughter asked about vario u s religions she said, "We are all the sa me, right? We all love God?" I said, "They all are going to split hell w ide open! Done! Conversation's over. These are cults. None of them worship Jesus Christ." She wondered what makes us different and I told her, "We are believers in him who died and rose again. Only one

God died and rose again. His name is Jesus Christ. Out of that whole class, you are the only bo rn-aga in, tongueta l kin g believer that I k now of. You are the only Christian." Here is the commandment. "None of those other groups will make it to heaven, unless they meet your God." At that moment I turned on the news and star ted listening. She reached up slowly and turned it down. She asked, "My friend is not going to hea ven?" I said, "If she does not meet Jesus, she will not go to hea ven. Keep this in mind. You have been raised to serve Jesus Christ, the only true and living God." That commandment is now etched in my daughter's mind. According to scripture, she will sleep it, walk it, and hear it until Jesus comes. She will always remember it.

Proverbs 7:1, *"My Son, you keep my words, and lay up my commandments with thee."* I often tell that to my son to "remember what I said" before he leaves to go back to college. We go out into the living room, and we bless him and we pray over *him*. One day, before my son lef t for a road trip, I asked him, Who's driving?" "We are all taking turns," my son responded. Then I gave him a commandment. "Make sure to keep the nuts from behind the wheel!" He started to say, "Well, dad, every body..." I interjected once again, "and you keep the nuts from behind the wheel!" Then I gave another co mmandment. "You keep your room under control." He said, "There will be four of us in a room." I repeated, "You keep your room under control. You do not let a ny stupidity go on in that room. If you do not like what is happening, you either put them out or you call me, and you will get your own room." My son walked up into the room one night and they had some foul perversion on the television. He said, "Fellas, this cannot go on in this room." Instantly, they turned it off! They said, "What are we all going to do then?" He said, "You want to go out and eat? Do you want to swim in the pool? Do you want to go for a walk down the boulevard to see some of the lights in this tow n? We cannot have that on inside this room." The Bible says, We should have dominion. I have always told my son, "You dominate! You do not walk in the room and be number five or number three. You are number one every time you walk into the room. You dominate the situation. Take advantage of the doors God has opened, and do no t let anybody push you around. You be the man every single time!" I believe in being a leader, not a f ollower.

Proverbs 7:7 *"And behold among the simple ones, I discerned among tile youths, a young man void of understanding."* He was void of what? Understanding. I tell you for a fact; it is scriptura l, and it is truth- a woman cannot fulfill a man's role in the house and a man cannot fulfill a woman's. If a person claims, "I am a single parent in the house, and I am fulfilling both roles," he is lying to himself, to God, and to the church. The best thing a single mother can do is to try to find a man who can impact her children occasionally. He can be a married man, but make sure it is all right with his w ife. If a mother tries to fulfill both roles, she will come up short. The reason they call God "El Shaddai" is because it means that he is the many-breasted one. God is able to be a father and a mother, yet he calls himself father because we need the spirit of the Father. It is important to remember that when he created us in the garden, he created two of us. It is impossible for me to be "Mr. Mom." A single man, with children can ask, "Brother is it all right if I just ask your wife to talk to my kids from time to time?" They need a mother's voice. There are elemen ts in women of gentleness, sweetness, and sof tness that are not in men. I travel out of town sometimes. When I come home from one of my trips, everyone from the twenty-one-year-old down to the twelve year old was having a big ca mpout in my bedroom. I walked in and said, "What's going on? I am home now. Nobody is sleepi ng in here except my wife and me." There is so mething a bout the n u rturing aspect of the mother.

One of my children said to me, "I get scared, Daddy, when you are not home. I have got to stay in Mom's room." W hen I am there, they can sleep in their room. The interestin g thin g is that they sleep downstai rs. My wife and 1 a rc upstairs. Yet, when my wife is gone, they are not scared. They apparently believe that i can get downstairs in enough time to protect them.

When my wife is gone, nobody is uncomfortable because there is a spirit in the house from the father. It ma kes a statement, "You do not have to worry a bo ut anything."

Proverbs 7:11-15 *"She was loud and stubbom; her feet abide not in her hou se; now is she without, now in the streets, and lieth in ·wait at every corner."* I tell my wife that I run my church the same way I run my house. 1 run both of them th ro ugh certa in Bi blical principles. I can correct somebody at church just Like I correct somebody at home and not be mad or upset. I am obligated to give commandments a n d bring correction. With my children, I am never mad. I will correct them, set the structure, pick up, and move on.

It is necessary for the f ather to speak and impart

information. Tho u gh the mother gives instruction and direction through the word of God, the father issues commandments. The only ones who give commandments in the entire Bi ble are kings and fathers-people who teach wisdom. It is interesting that God ranked fathers right next to kings.

Commandments of the Father

Chapter 4

"My son, keep my words, and lay up my commandments with thee. Keep my command ments, and live my law as the apple of thine eye." Proverbs 7:1-2

The Bible says that the father gives the command ments and the mother gives the law. The law is the Word of God. The father, because it comes from his spirit, brings instruction by way of commandment. While it is similar, it comes out of his spirit, by direction of commandments not discussion. A father does not usually try to reason; he simply issues a commandment. Looking in the Word of God at the spirit of the father and the commanding process, the father has the ability to set your life in a direction of success or destruction.

In essence when your father or a man that is in a father role begins to speak into your life as a commandment, it can either destroy you, or help you to succeed.

"All these nre the twelve tribes of Israel and this is whnt their father spake unto them and bless them everyone according to his blessing, he blesses them." He charged them and said unto them, "I am to be gathered unto my people; bury me with my fathers inn cnve that is in the field of Ephron the Hittite." Genesis 49:28-29

"There they buried Abraham and Sarah his wife; there they buried Isaac and Rebekah Iris wife; and there I buried Lenh. The pu rcllnse of the field nnd of the cave thnt is therein wns from the children of Hetlr. And when]ncob lrnd mnrle nn end of commanding Iris sons, Ire gathered up his feet into the bed, nnd yielded up the ghost, and was gathered unto Iris people." Genesis 49: 31-33

"And jacob called unto his sons, and said, 'gather yourselves together, that I may tell you that which shall befall you in the last days." Genesis 49:1

There are certain things that a father has a right to release and they all come out of his spirit. So who we would love to receive from is a Bible-based, prayerful, spiritual man, living holy before God.

Looking back at how the spirit of Moses came upon the seventy, and highlighting the fact that Elisha asked for the spirit of Elijah in the Old Testament, it is clear that there is a need for a father to speak into the lives of his children and make command ments to them. Now we are examining in the Word of God, that a father tends not to discu ss his commandments. It is not his role to convince or to get them to understand. He makes a commandment with the sole purpose of launching them in a positive direction. Jacob, or Israel, gathered the twelve tribes of Israel; gathered his twelve sons together to ma ke father-like commandments.

> *"Reuben, thou art my firstborn, my might, and the beginning of my strength, the excellency of dignity, and the excellency of power; Unstable as water, thou shalt not excel; because thou wen test up to thy father's bed; then defiledst thou it; he went up to my couch."* Genesis 49:3

Jacob told Reuben, that he would not amount to anything!

> *"Simeon and Leviare brethren; instruments of cruelty are* in *their habi tations. Omy soul, come not thou into their secret; unto thei r assembl y, mine honor, be not thou united; for in their anger they slew a man, and in their self-will, they digged down a wall. Cursed be their anger, for it was fierce; and thei r wrath, forit was cruel; I will divide them in Jacob, and scatter them in Israel.* Genesis 49:5-7

Jacob takes a position not as a prophet, but as a father. A father has the right to set the course of his child's life under God so he either succeeds or fails..." It shows you the power in the spoken word of a father. This was supposed to be a day of rejoicing, but he told both of them, that they would be divided and scattered.

> *"Judah, thou art he whom thy brethren shalt praise; thy lwnd shall be in the neck of thine enemies; thy father's children shall bow down before thee. Judah* is *a Lion's whelp; from thy prey, my son, thou art gone up; he stooped down, he couched down as a lion, and as an old lion; who shall rouse him up? The scepter shall not depart from Judah, nor a lawgiver from between his feet, until Shiloh come; and unto him shall the gathering of the people be. Judah, you ·will defeat your enemies.* Genesis 49:8-10

Jacob gave discouraging news to the first two, but told Judah he will be victorious! He commanded that Judah's own family will bow down to hjm. Jacob released this out of his spirit into Judah's life. Jacob spoke by way of commandment. This was not a prophetic move, though it is looked at as one, he actually declared the failure or the success of his own sons.

Genesis 49:13 *"Zebulun shall dwell at the haven of the sea; and he shall be for an haven of ships; and his border shall be unto Zidon."* Jacob sets Zebulun up in some kind of a shipping company. Commandments do not come in the form of long discussions. It can be offensive sometimes when a father says, "Just do it." But, when a Godly, blood-washed, spirit-filled individual speaks from a father's perspective, as long as you trust the voice, there should not be a lot of discussion. One mjght think, "I am grown/" but that is the problem. We bring the nature of the world inside the kingdom, and when something is said to us, we want to debate or discuss it. We do not lose our freewill, but if a father speaks out of his spirit and releases something, we must realize the potential that is in that individual. Therefore, simply take on the role of a sponge, absorb something, and glean something. I want to have my spirit open so that I am able to receive something from the individua l servin g in a father's role. Zebulun will have an importexport business d ow n by the ocean and business opportunities will brea k forth.

I had a preacher in the office recently, and I gave him advise on *his* dress. He dressed very casuall y, and I said, "As long as you dress that casually, you will al ways be preaching on the street comer, *which* is great, if you want to be a street corner preacher. I helped him to beat the head ache of preaching on the corner by giving him this adv ice. I explained to him how to act and dress himself appropriately. "Always," I told him, "be respectful, and realize that somebody has been doing this longer than you have, and you will be just fine and dandy."

Sometimes, because of the anoi nting on our lives, we do not want to hear anything, and no one can give us advice. However, always someone as more oil. We must have an ear to hear. I can look at someone and say to myself, "My God, I can preach better than that! I would have had the pl ace screa ming by now. I could have taken the message and..." Yet, what I need to do is to look at what they have accomplished. I might have had the place screa ming, and I may have been able to do certain things better, but I mu st realize that God ordained them to be in their position. Since they are there, I should just be still and listen. Fathers are in roles to take us to the nex t level and platf orm. Though it is not a l wa ys easy to hear, I want listen to what the fathers have to say because it is going to propel me to my next place in Jesus' name.

I believe if we are sensitive to hear subtle instructions that the Spirit of the Lord gives us, we are able to go hi gher and deeper into the things of God through the commandments of the fathers.

We sometimes react to situations with fear. We put up walls, and find ourselves pushin g o thers away. We find ourselves having difficulty und erstanding and feel as if everything said is intended to destroy u s rather than build us up. Fathers in the spirit many times speak in parables. These commandments hold earthly meaning that comes from a heavenly source, we are wise to listen. Let's ask the Spirit of God to help change our minds so we can speak the right things and flow in the right things.

Heirs of the Father

Chapter 5

"And the Lord visited Sarah as he had said, and the Lord did unto Sarah as he had spoken. For Sarah conceived, and bare Abraham a son in his old age, at the set time of which God had spoken to him. And Abraham called the name of the son that was born unt him, Sarah bare to him, Isaac. And Abraham circumcised Isaac being eight days old, as God had commanded him. And Abraham was an hundred years old, when his son Isaac was born unto him. And Sarah said, God hath made me to laugh, so that all who hear will laugh with me. A nd she said, who would have said unto Abraham, that Sarah should have given children suck? For I have born him a son in his old age." Genesis 21:1-7

The name Isaac also means, "laugh." It is clear that God has a sense of humor. We are looking at the father's realm and I want to share what I consider to be the three sons of Abraham. The Bible is clear that Abraham is "the father of many nations." He has three primary sons.

> *Genesis 17:1-7 "When Abram was ninety years old and nine (a year before Isaac showed up), the Lord appeared unto Abram and said unto him, I am the Almighty God; walk before me and be thou perfect. And I will make my covenant between me and thee, and I will multiply thee exceedingly.' And Abram fell on his face: and God talked with him, saying, as for me, 'Behold, my covenant is with thee and thou shalt be a father of many nations. Neither shall thy name be called anymore, Abram, but thy name shall be Abraham; for a father of many nations have I made thee. And I will make thee exceeding fruitful, and I will make nations of thee, and kings shall come out of thee. And I will establish my covenant between me and thee and thy seed after thee..."'*

The blessings of Abraham are flowing down to his children and even his grandchildren. So Abraham's seed is going to prosper because of their original daddy. So we want daddy to always be in a proper state of ex istence. Once aga in, many have difficulty receiving from those who are in the spiritual role of a father. They have difficulty receiving from the spirit of the father because their earthly fathers were psychotic, out of control, ungodly or perverted. Therefore, when so meone reaches out and gives them a hand to try give them direction, they of ten cannot embrace it because they are remembering previous experiences. We need to realize that there are certain blessings flowing from certain spiri tually ordained positions or relationships, and we want to embrace them. Genesis 12:1 *"Now the Lord had said unto Abram, get thee ou t of thy country, and from thy kindred and from thy father's hou se."* God wanted to deal with Abram one on one and make him a father of nations.

> *"And I will make of thee a great nation, and I will bless thee, and make thy name great; and thou shalt be a blessing. And I will bless them that bless thee, and curse him that curseth thee; and in thee shall all of tile falllilies of the earth be bles sed."* Genesis 12:2

He is releasing certain blessin\ gs through the realms of Abraham unto his seed and ca using certain breakthroughs to come forth from a fatherly position.

> *"That in blessing I will bless thee, and in multiplying I will multiply thy seed as the stars of heaven, and as the sand which* is *upon the sea shore; and thy seed shall possess the gate of his enemies."* Genesis 22:17

One of the translations of that is to: defeat, *domi*nate, take a uthority ov`er, and control the gates of the enemy. Genesis 22:18 *"And in thy seed shall all the nations of the earth be blessed; because thou hast obeyed my voice."* Through Abraham's chil dren, there is a blessing coming.

> *"Now Sarai Abraham's wife bare him no children; and she had an handmaid, an Egyptian whose*

> *name was Hagar. And Sarai said unto Abraham, behold now, the Lord hath restrained me from bearing; I pray thee, go in unto my maid; it may be that I may obtain children by her. And Abram harkened unto the voice of Sarai."* Genesis16:1-2

> *"And Sarai, Abram's wife took Hagar her maid the Egyptian,(Egypt means the world) after Abraham had dwelt ten years in the land of Canaan, and gave her to her husband Abram to be his wife."* Genesis 16:3

They had lived in Canaan for ten years. The number ten symbolizes fear, doubt, and unbelief. Sarah and Abraham were uncertain as to whether or not God was going to show up. Sarai then began to look to the world for her help.

> *"And Sarni said into Abram, My wrong be upon thee: I have given my maid into thy bosom; and when she saw that she had conceived, I was despi sed in her eyes: the Lord judge behoeen me and thee."* Genesis 16:5

So Abram told Sarai that if she did not like what was going on, she could throw Hagar out of the ca mp.

> *"And an angel of the Lord said unto her (Hagar), L will multiply thy seed exceed ingly, that it simi/ not be numbered for multitude."* Genesis 16:10

The name Ishmael means, "God will hear." God heard the cry of Ha gar, so that the blessings of the father would come down upon Ishmael.

> *"After these things, the Word of the Lord came unto Abram in a vi sion saying, fear not, Abram: I am thy shield, and thy exceeding great reward." And Abram said, "Lord, God, what wilt thou give me, seeing that I go childless and the steward of my house is Eliezer of Damascus." And Abram said, "Behold to me thou has not given no seed; and, lo, the one born in my hou se in my heir." And, behold, the word of the Lord ca me unto him saying, "This shall not be thine heir, but he that shall come forth out of thine own bowels shall be thine heir." And he brought him forth abroad and said, "look now toward heaven, and tell the stars, if thou be able to number them... so ·will thou seed be."* Genesis 15:1

The name Eliezer means, "God is my helper." He has one legal child, Isaac. He also has another son Ishmael. Now you have to remember that Abraham was not just a man, but a prophet, and as we know, what prophets s poke, ca me to pass. Abra ha m says, three hundred pi us men were born in his house. Every body in a father's house is his c hild. A ll of those three hund red men were his children. The men of war that Abraham trained himself were his children. Isaac, Ishmael the ha lf-son, and those that were no t even his by natural seed were his children by spiritual connection and all have a right to the promises of God. Everybody that is born un to his house became a son.

The Father in heaven is not a respecter of persons. A real father is not a respecter of persons. All of the children a retreated the same. That is why whe n the prodiga l's brother got upset and said, "You never killed a goat for me," the father *said*, "We could have killed one anytime. You did not ask." A true father wa nts to see all of his children succeed. Success is different in each pe r on's life. Success to one is a studio a partment. Success to another is five acres of l and with ten bedrooms and six bathrooms.

Here is a scenario **I** went through with my own cluldren. I called the school f or progress reports. One of my children came home and said, "I'm sorry, Da ddy. My a verage is only a ninety-six this qu a rter." I said, "I bless you for your ninety-six percent. My other child ca me home and she a l ways wa nts to give me a bi g explanation before she shows me her progress report, but her average grade usually is around a seventy-eight percent. r said to both of them, "Did both of you try your best?" They both said, "Yes." I said, "I am ha ppy tonight! lee crea m for everybod y!" A father just wa nts to see su ccess. He does not want to see brain surgeons all over the house. He does not ex pect to see everyone become a millionaire. He just wants everyone to enjoy his or her life and be successful! His greatest pleasure is to be able to bless them all and to be openhearted enough tra in them all.

Bo th Ga latians 4:28 and Galatians 4:6-7 spea k to sons regarding promises.

> *"Wherein God, willing more abundantly to show unto the heirs of promise tile immutability of his counsel, confirmed it by an oath..."*
> Hebrews 6:17

God wants to show unto the hei rs a promise. You can say that you are a Son of God. I am a Son of God, too, but I am a son of Abra ham also. The Word of God says that a n heir has promises. Abra ha m ha d over three hundred heirs that he had trained himself. That is what fathers do. Fathers shou ld train their children. I tra ined my daughter to drive before she went to driving school.

> *"By faith he sojourned in the land of promise, as in a strange country, dwelling in tabernacles with I saac and Jacob, the hei rs with him of the same promise."* Hebrews 11:9

We are examining the promises that transcend generations. We have to look at it from a positive perspective rega rding the promises of God. We cannot overlook the negative aspec ts as well. That is why some poeple became drunkards because their daddy's were drunka rds. Samuel's sons were sinful. He did not teach them to be sinful. He was a great man of God, Samuel. Why were his sons sinful? They took *it* from Samuel's spiritua l daddy. Whatever was there fro m past generations came down the line. So there is a need to be careful in all dimensions of life and to watch and to see from whence blessings and curses flow down. My heavenly father's promises should come here. Spiritua l father's promises hould come here as well into our lives and into our hearts so that changes can take place.

I know an electrician. I do not know anything about electricity. I tried to do an electrical job once and almost burned the house down. When you do not know certain things, you have to get somebody that understands it. I love when I go into a hospital and see folks arguing down doctors. I say to myself, "Then why are you here, then?" If you know so much, then why are you here?" This is what happens in the kingdom a lot of times. Here comes God releasing spiritual principles, revelations, promises, etc., and instead of just embracing them and understanding their source, we have a controversial stance because we think that we know something.

A lot of times because of our own pride, we do not want anyone to tell them anything. I believe that one reason people do not want people to tell us any thing is because we have been hurt, or taken advan tage of. Perhaps you took someone's advice in the past and the situation did not work out well. Therefore we adopt a frame of mind that we *are* going to do things ourselves, and there is a mentality that we wou ld rather fail trying than fail with someone's help. But you have got to get some help from somewhere. Hebrews 6:12 *"That ye be not slothful, but followers of them who through faith and patience inherit the promises."*

Hebrews 12:7 *"If ye endure chastening, God dealeth with you as with sons; for what son is he whom the father chasteneth not?"* Most of us do not like being corrected. However, once you come into the family, you are going to get corrected at one time or another. I believe that this spirit of the father brings a balance. Every body gets the same kind of loving. Everybody gets the same kind of treatment. Every body gets the same kind of hugs, same kind of touch, and the same kind of discipline. The problem is that we are so bound sometimes with fears a bout someone ta king advantage of us that we put up walls. A great thing to do in the kingdom is to have a mindset that embraces change! Keep your eyes focused on what you are coming ou t of and w here you are planning o n going now. The q uestion that should be in the forefront of your mind is, w here is God taking me now and is my spirit open? When your spirit is open, an anointing can be released from your spiritual father over your life. When you yield to the Holy Spirit, you will be amazed where you will end up! But it is a matter of pulling down walls!

Proper Instruction From The Father

Chapter 6

Here is a thought for you. There is a need to h ear what your daddy ha s to say. Whe n fathers start speaking, there is a need for youto listen to what they are saying. The bible says that you will no t be destroyed if you listen to the instru ctions of your father. The bible says that you will not be mangled or twisted. You will not go off in the wrong direction. You will not find chaotic circumstances of life ove rwhelming you if you listen to your father's instructions. I know it may be diffic ult. In this wonderful society of ours, we have this belief that we are grown already (no matter our age). I do not really believe that a l ot of us are grown. It is just that we have been fo rced to live the life of an adult prematurely due to a lack of gu idance and instruction. The wonder of the bible, however, is that somebody has inf ormation f or you. When fathers love their children and children love their fathers, then these children should be able to listen to some instruction from their fathers. I know it is hard to listen to instruction, especially when we beheve that we know something and we are grown.

Yet, if I can listen to information and instruction from a father, it will give me commandments that contain wisdom. Now if the sons and dau ghters wou ld only listen, ha lf of the headache of their father's life would be resolved. Half of the iss u es that were trying to trouble you woul d be wiped out through the voice of your father.

In 1Samuel 2:12-27 the Word of God says that the law of the Levites or the priests says that when the people ca me to make sacrifices, they would throw their meat into the pot. That is how the priests survived back then. They would throw this three-pronged flesh hook into the pot and stir it around. Whatever the flesh hook grabbed belonged to the preachers.

Eli was the priest at that time. Unfortunately Eli was a backslidden priest. When a daddy backslides, he does not i nteract with his children properly. He just lets them go in whatever direction they choose, instead of givin g them sound spiritual instr uction. Eli was raised as a man of God, (although now backslidden). The scripture states that the sons of Eli did not even worship Jehova h Jireh. They were working for their daddy, but they did not take his instruc tion. This was primarily because he was very old and frail, so they just did whatever they wanted to do.

The Word of God ma kes a statement that they would go into the temple and tell the people not to put the meat in the pot. They would tell the people to just hand it over to the sons because they claimed that they wa nted the fresh meat. If the peo ple refused, they w ould threaten to ta ke it by force. That was interesting, I thought. Why would they get so aggressive with the poeple? It could only be due to the fact that they had no fatherly instruction. Instead of the father standing up and living a Godly life and giving them instructions on how to move forward, he backed away. The father became very reserved and he backslid. Eli regressed in his relationship with God and with his children, and the problems began. The Israelites began not to come to the temple the way they should. They began to w i thdraw from the temple and from the priests because the sons of Eli were committing all of these illegal acti o ns. All of a sudden, one day a prophet ca me to Eli and said, "Listen, if you do not get your house in order, God is going to judge you and your children." This is the shortened version of the pro phecy. Get you r house in order or you w ill be judged! This whole situation started because daddy was not in his proper post. If daddy gets jud ged for his incompetence, it filters down unto the children. Of course we know the passage, "Israel goes to war one day" and because his two sons Hophni and Phinehas are not acting Godly, both of them are killed in battle. The a rc of the covena nt is ta ken a way. The Word of God sa ys that Eli, when he hears this news, is sitting at the gate of the temple w here the fathers a lways sat. He sat there and hea rd that his sons were dead and that the a rc was missing and it so overwhelms him that he falls backwards, brea ks his neck, and dies. All of this is from a man who knew God, but refu sed to continue in his Godly behav ior and to instruct his sons.

Sometimes we as fathers do no t want to ta ke on all of the pressure of instructing our children. We have adopted a rnindset that they are grown. Let them do what they wa nt to do. I do not have the time. I am trying to work out my own soul's salvation. Father's, listen to me. You are supposed to be saved and mature now. So, as a father, you are supposed to be giving: instruc ti on, insight, understanding, and comprehension into your sons and dau g hte rs. Mea nwhile, Proverbs says that the children are waiting for: the instruction, the wisdom, and the insight of their fathers. When they do not get the instruction, the wisdom, and the i nsight, it says that the children are judged, fall to the wayside and are destroyed.

1 Kings13 is a wonderful passage. A young prophet came to town and prophesied to the king. When he prophesied to the king, the king did not like the prophecy and the young prophet said, "Your hand will whither up!" The king's hand withered up. The king said, "Help me! Help me, young prophet!" The young prophet ministered unto him and his hand was made whole. He was so overw helmed that he said, "Stay at my house. Eat, drink, and stay here tonight." The young prophet's response was, "I cannot eat here. I cannot sleep here. I cannot drink here." The Lord said, "Don't eat, drink, or sleep here and do not leave the same way you come in. Leave in a different direction." The young prophet then lef t town. He had shaken the entire city. Everybody heard about this young prophet. An old man of God heard a bout this young pro phet through his children and the commotion in the street. He heard that a young man of God had turned the city upsidedown. The old man of God said, "Saddle my ass quickly. I have to find this prophet."

He f ound the young prophet outside of the city under a tree, resting. The old man said, "Listen, I am a prophet also. Since we are both prophets, you need to spend some time and eat with me. The young prophet said, "No, that is not so. The Lord told me do not eat, do not drink, and do not return to this place. Do not sleep in this place and leave in a different way than you ca me in." The old man said, "An a n gel ca me to me and told me that thou ar t to stay at my house tonight." The young prophet with a trusting and open hea rt went to the old man's house. While he was at the old man of God's house, the Spirit of the Lord comes upon the old Prophet. He bega n to pro phecy, Thus saith the Lord: because you have eaten in this place, and drank in this place, and have not left this place (when L told you not to eat, no t to drink, and not to stay in this place), thou shalt die and no t see the graves of thy fathers." The young man of God was out of *his* mind wi th a nger and shame. "Oh my God! How could you do such a thing to me?" The old man of God did not know what to say because he knew he did wrong. The young man of God hastily ran out of the house and f orgo t the Word of the Lord, "Do not l eave the way you came in." The bible said, "On the road, a lion meets him." If you know anything about lions, lions do not kill unless they are hungry. The young prophet was killed by the li on. The lion never ate the body, however. The old man of God was i n erro r, and he lead the young prophet dow n the path of error as well.

The greatest thing that the old man of God could have done was to have taken on a fatherhood position with the young prophet. He should not have tried to be a pro phe t of equal standing with him; "I am a prophet also." It would have been greater for him to rea li ze, that, "I am your father, son. I realize that you cannot eat, drink, or sleep here. I just wa nt to say that I am prou d of what you did today here. Get home safely. Whenever you come through again, you have omewhere to stay" (as a father doe). He never did that, thou gh. He allowed himsel f to become caught up into the exci temen t of wan ting to be recognized also. When he did that, he end angered the life of the young prophet to the point that the young prophet died. He disrespected what God was trying to do.

When a father is present, or the spirit of a father in a man, he is never threatened by the son. He always pushes him into greatness. He should have pushed that young prophet that d ay, but instea d his interference caused the young prophet to lose his very life. Fathers are not threatened by their sons. Every father wants his son to be greater than himself. Fathers do not try to hinder their sons, but fathers try to, as Prover bs says, "Give them instruction and insight that they might be preserved." We have examined two strange incidents in the Word of God. We began looking at 1 Samuel. Then we went through 1 Kings. Both times, men that were fathers did not step up because they did not want the press ure of fatherhood. They did not want the pressure of the father relationship. So in Eli's case, he simply shunned *his* sons. He did not interact with them. The boys were in drastic error, and he did not even bother to give them instruc tion. The bible said that the sons of Eli used to sl eep with women inside the House of God. Imagine the preacher's sons sleeping with young women inside the House of God. Eli never gave them instruction to try and save them.

The old man of God, in 1 Kings, interferes and causes the death of *his* spiritual sons because he was threatened (due to all of the attention on the young man of God). Proverbs 10:1 *"A wise son mnkeh a glad father, but a foolish son is a heaviness of his mother."* Every daddy wants his son to make him glad. If a father gives instruction, your son will make you glad. I am not saying that your son is going to agree with everything you say, but at least speak! When you speak, in the back of his mind, that commandment will come to his remembrance. Do not "browbeat" him, but give him information. So gladness is coming to you if you speak to your son. If you think, "he does not want to hear what I have to say," it does not matter. Say it a nyway! In the book of Ezekiel, it talks about the fact that you do not wa nt the "blood of the people" on your hands. If you do not speak, when you know that so mething is wrong, the blood of the people that come to harm will be upon you. If you spea k when you see that something is wrong, even if they do not like it, you are free from their blood.

Proverbs 13:1 *"A wise son hears his father's instructions, but a scorner heareth not rebuke."* Sometimes you have to rebuke and correct your son. "Son, do not do it that way." He does not have to like it. He could be offended. Your daughter could be offended. "Daughter, do not wear that dress. Do not stay out at that party until two in the morning." They could be offended. You cannot make everybody happy. However, at least you are giving input.

The first point is this: the fathers, you better talk if you want to be glad. The second point is that sometimes when you talk, you have to give correction! Here is an interesting thing. When I spea k to people even within the church family, there are times when I say, "Take my i nstruction, do it and be blessed." The first point is that God wants you fathers to be glad and to give instr uctions. The second point is that God wants your children to be able to receive the rebuke and to make you glad. Children are not going to be able to receive the rebuke if you do not give the rebuke. You have to be able to give correction. Keep in mind that you are not their brother. You are not their friend. You are their daddy. You have a big responsibility.

The last point of the three is stated in Proverbs 15:5 *"A fool des pises instruction, but he that regardeth reproff is prudent."* A child that listens to your instruction makes you glad. Sometimes children think that they have all the answers. Just talk to your children. That is all you have to do. The problem is that we do not want to talk. You are a daddy. You have to open your mouth and say something. Everybody is not going to listen. Everybody is not going to like it. Some people are going to think that you are out of control, or trying to be a big shot. You know what the problem is? I am a big shot! I am the daddy or the father, si I can give some instruction to my children to help them go forward in life.

You have to talk to one child softly and talk to another one sternly, and give yet another one regulations. But at the end of the day, I want to sleep when I go to bed at night. So I am going to talk to all of my children. I have one at the university and three at home. I talk because my job is to rescue them and give them instruction.

Forgiveness Of The Father

Chapter 7

Proverbs 30:11 *"There is a generation that curseth their father and doth not bless their mother.* Psalms 103:13 *"Like a father pitieth his children, so the Lord pitieth them that fear hint."* A father will pity *his* children. He feels bad for what they are going through because he loves them. Our father in hea ven pities u s and pities the foolish mistakes that we make. The father is concerned enou gh to contemplate, "How can I get them out of this fix?"

Reflecting back on the story of the prodigal son, we see that not once was the prodigal so n's father angry. He felt sad. When the son came home, the father embraced the child and loved on the child. There is a sorrow that comes from fathers because they care about the well being of their children and they wan t to see them progress and become greater than themselves. Let's examine Jesus' disposition before *hi s* crucifixion on the cross. Luke 23:34 states that then said Jesus, *"Father forgive them, for they know not what they do."* Why did Jesus have to say that? That statement stems from the fact that the father is a forgiver. A father is always making himself available. A father has a forgiving spirit. My w ife and I were counseling one day a man and we realized that he was ma d all the time! He said, "She gave that boy of mine the last Twinkie a couple of weeks ago." I said, "You must be joking!" He said, "Listen, it is hard working o ut there. You do not know w hat it is to work in Florida (out in the heat) at a construction sight. It is hard work! I hid that Twinkie inside the shelf. I do not care if there was nothing for the boy to eat. I was going to get him some Burger King. How did she give that Twinkie to that boy? The woman disrespects me!" I said, "My God, the man needs deliverance." He said, "You do not understand." I said, "I do no t understand at all because everything you h a ve, you give to your children. If the boy is hungry and **all** you have is a Twinki e, give the boy a Twinkie. Since tod ay is payday, go buy five more boxes of Twinkies if you like.

The child was not ten years old. That is something that a lways stuck out in my mind. The man was angry and unforgiving over a Twinkie.

We can take that example from the Twinkie realm to maybe the child running up the phone bill. Instead, perhaps the child forgot to lock the door. Maybe he forgot to bring the garbage pails inside. Then, the wind took them down the street. No matter what the situation, we as fathers are supposed to forgive. We do not realize the power of a godly man. When he does not forgive, it brea ks the spirit of his children. Phrases like, "you are not a ny good," or "you will not amount to anything," are damaging! Even if you see your *chil*dren mess up four, five and six times, you forgive them. You embrace them. You tell them, let's start again. There is a need to forgive!

According to scr ipture, a godly father who is unforgiving can put his child in bondage. Remember the story of Jaco b when Jacob gathered all of his sons, and he cursed so me of them? When speaking to his eldest son, he stated that, "You will never be any good! You are going to be like the sea, tossed back and forth." If you search, that is what they became. Whatever daddy said, that is what they became. He spoke to one and said that he was going to be invol ved in the import and ex por t business. One was to mingle with royalty. He could have looked beyond their situations and difficulti es. Poeple make mistakes. Children mess up because nobody has all the a nswers and we are aJl lea rning through this process of life.

If you tell the m, it still does not get through a lot of times. For exa mple, if you tell them the following: 1) Do not stick that nail in that electrica l socket or you will fry yoursel f and drop dead. 2) Use drugs and it will fry your brain cells. 3) Drink alcohol and it will damage your liver. If you tell them these things, of ten the message still does not get through to them. Yet after they have fallen and end up in some kind of tro uble, the father does not read them the riot act. The father forgives them. There is a need to release. There is a need to forgive because forgiveness brings healing.

Women are more emotion a l than men. It is not a negative. It is just a statement. When the Bible says that the woman is the weaker vessel, it is not referring to a spiritual or a physical weakness. It is referring to the emotional realm. Things hurt them deeper and they withdraw farther from an incident. That is where a good, Holy Ghost filled father comes in, and assumes his role. He can heal the wound. Statements like, "I beli eve in you. I am sorry you went through this. Every thin g is going to be fine." Encou ragement comes forth to build us up both male and female. He released his spirit upon them and it changes, restores, and builds them up In Jesus' name. There is a healing from the forgiving presence of the father.

> *"And AbrahamI journeyed from thence toward the sou th countrv and dwelled between Kadesh and Shur, and sojourned* in *Gerar. And Abraham said of Sarah,* his *wife,'She is my sister;' and Abimelech king of Gerar sent, and took Sarah. But God came to Abimelech in a dream by night, and said to him, 'Behold, thou art but a dead man, for the woman with thou has taken; for she* is *a man's wife."'* Genesis 20: 1-3

Sa ra h must have been a fine-looking woman although the Word says that she was ninety years old. Thats hows the power of God. The Word says Abimelech took her and brought her into his house and God says to Abimilech in a dream, in essence, you are as good as a dead man because you touched ano ther man's wife.

> *"But Abimelech had not come near her; and said, 'Lord, would you slay also a righteous nation? Said Ire not unto me, she* is *my sister? ...Even she herself said he is my brother; in the integrity of my heart and the innocence of my hand s have I done this.' God said unto him in a dream, 'Yea,*

I know tlrat thou didst this in the integrity of thine heart; for I also witheld thee from sinning against me; therefore, suffered I thee not to touch her.'" Genesis 20: 3-6

I tell you we serve a good God. God said I stopped you from touching the woman. That is the amazing thing about God. Even before you come into the kingdom and begin going into the wrong direction, God still sends help ahead of hme because he is trying to change your life. What a great God!

"Now therefore restore the man his wife; for he is *a prophet, and he shall pray for thee, and thou salt live; and if thou restore her not, know that thou shall surely die, thou and all that are thine. Therefore Abimelech rose early in the morning, and called all his servants, and told all these things in their ears; and the men were sore afraid. Then Abimelech called Abraham, and said unto him,'What ha st thou done unto us? What have fended thee, that thou hast brought on me and on my kingdom great sin?'" thou hast done deed s unto me that ought not to be done.* Genesis 20:7-9

"And Abimelech said, Behold, my land is before thee. Dwell where it pleaseth thee. And unto Sarah he said, 'Behold I hath given thy brother, a thousand pieces of silver; behold he is to thee a covering to thy eyes, unto all that are with thee, and with all other;' thus she was reproved. So Abraham prayed unto God; and God healed

Abimelech and his wife, and his maidservants, and they bare children. For the Lord had fast closed up all of tile wombs of Abimelech, because of Sarah, Abrnham's wife." Genesis 20:15-18

Now we rea d a short while ago that Abraham means the "father of many nations." According to what we are reading, this father forgave these people. The wombs of every woman in that city were closed. No one co uld have any children. It says sickness ca me into the land. When the father in heaven and even the father in the earthly realm (Abraham, the father of many n ations), forgave this man and prayed a prayer over them, all of the wombs of these women opened back up! They were once again able to conceive. Healing had come into the land. God had manifested himself because the father had shown forgiveness! Where there is forgiveness, there is healing.

When a father will not forgive, it brings bondage. No matter what mistakes we have made, the father will a l ways forgive us. Even when we do some thing that the father does not like, he still forgives us. When we do something knowingly or unknowi ngl y, the father still forgives us. Fathers are *alwa ys* there forgiving and forgiving! God is not like Noah. Do you recall when Ham saw his na kedness and Noah cursed him? God sees us make mistakes and he keeps on forgiving because there is healing power in forgiving! Fathers do not hold things over our heads. They release us through love.

When Abraham prayed for Abimelech and the whole city, everybody was healed. Can you imagine? He did not call him a father. He called him prophet. Imagine if the prophet cursed them? Instead of cursing them, he f orgave them. This is the positio n and the power that is in the spirit of the father that was created under the hands of the Almighty God. Sometimes we fail to see these things. When we take on a father role, we do not understand the ability to release people. That is why when the Bible says when you repute sin to poeple, it is on them. If you forgive it then it leaves them.

> *"After thi s manner, therefore pray ye, our father who art in heaven, hallowed be thy name. Thy kingdom come. Thy will be done on earth as it* is *in heaven. Give us this day our daily bread and forgive us..."* Matthew 6:9

Is it not interesting that we are asking our heavenly father to forgive? It is trying to show us that everything repeats after its kind. The Bible says in Genesis 1:11-12, 21,24-25, *"Everything after its kind."* So are not the fathers in the earthly realm supposed to impersonate, imitate, or mimic the father in the heavenly realm? If he can forgive us, what reason do we have for not forgiving our brethren? "Forgive us this day, forgive us this day..." we are dealing with a daily issue. "And forgive us our debts as we forgive our debtors." So there is a need for forgiveness. Let us look at Matthew 6:14. *"For if ye forgive men their trespasses, your heavenly father will also forgive you. But if you forgive not men their trespasses, neither will your heavenly father forgive you."*

A father walks around saying, "I am tired of that boy. If you want to invite him to Thanksgiving, you can in vite him to Thanksgiving, but I am tired of him." He is wrong! He cannot be tired of him! I am the seed of my father. No matter what I do, as l ong as my father is in the boundaries of creation, he is still forgiv ing me. I must be ready to always forgive. Now this principle spea ks very strongly to the father that if he does not forgive, then his father in heaven cannot forgive him. There is a forgiving process. Some times we do no t know the depths of the forgiving process.

I have a preacher friend that has difficulty in the area of forgiveness. In f act, he did n o t forgive his son (who came out of his loins) regarding one par ticular issue that ended up being very costly. What happened was that his son had applied to college. The college called his father for a reference. The father stated, "Well, I do not care what you do with him...do not send the records here..." So when he went dow n to that universi ty, do you know what they said to his son? "Sorry, you cannot come in here. I know that we said you were accepted. We made a mistake." The father had, in effect, branded him. Release the young man and set him free. You may be upset a bout a certain issue, but he is still your son. You have got to forgive him and release him. This is the good thing a bout Jesus. Jesus represents the father. Jesus said, *"The father and I are one. If you have seen me, you know you have seen the father."* Jesus was even moving in the nature of the spirit of the father. When Judas went to betray him in the garden, Jesus called to Judas, "Here comes my friend." He never c ursed Judas.

It says that Judas was tormented because of the evil act that he committed. The Word states that J udas took back the sil ver that he was given and still could not find peace. So he went ou t an d hung himself-not because the father was unf orgiving, but because he could not find peace. There is no sin that we could ever cornmit in the earthly realm that our wonderful Father does no t forgive. There is nothing we could do in the House of God fo r w hich the fathers of the Hou se cou ld not forgive us.

I remem ber we had an inci dent in here a while ago. I know why the man carne to church. He ca rne for women. We a ddressed it with him cordially and plainly. We said, "We love you, brother. We see you moving through the congregation. I know w hy you are here." He said, "Oh no, I am just having fellowship." So I said, "Then fellowship with the men." I said, "Brother, we see what you are doing. You are going to have to stop this thing." He said, "Well I am going to have to l eave." "No one said you are going to have to leave. We did not call your name from a platform. We did not even have a big meeting with you. Eyewitnesses have seen it and I have seen it for myself. I am just a pproaching you and asking you to stop making maneuvers on the sisters. Come and worship the true and living God. You are welcome anytime." He ended up lea ving the church. Now every time I see *him* on the street, I always embrace him and love on him.

What happened to him is that he became ashamed because he was ca ught. Though he is forgiven, he does not want to return. Now we could have not said a nything, then he would be jud ged by God. He was released and forgiven. So whether he returns here or goes somewhere else to worshi p, he is going to return somew here and serve the Lord and be blessed and go forwa rd in Jesus' name. That is the nature of a father... to forgive. Forgive and release. Forgive and release.

It is very unsettling to have so meo ne hold somethin g ove r your head. It is very much like being tormented. There are two individua l s that hold something over our head really well-someone who is upset wi th us and the devil. The dev il hold s the f act that we are Christians over our heads. He hates u s because we love God. A person that holds unforgiveness in their heart is holding some thin g over our heads. Unforgiveness hurts the one holding the unforgiveness the most. We are blessed in the name of the Lord because he is holding nothing over our heads. We are forgiven.

Ephesians 4:32 *"And be ye kind one to another, tenderhearted and forgiving one another."* You know how we learn to forgive? From the Father. I was ta lking to my wife a bout when I went to the Ca meroon's West Afr i ca and I was co unselin g all d ay. When I was counseling one d ay, a brother said, "Listen, I am so rry I hit my wife, but sometimes you just have to sla p them a little bit." Then he said, "You know that some women just like to be beat." I said, "You are being u sed by the d evil." I addressed it with him, rebuked him, ministered the l ove of Jesus to him, and then I said, "I need to let you know that you are forgiven." He then asked his wife for forgiveness and she forgave him.

Then I called the Pastor in. We addressed the issue with his pastor. His pastor was contemplating allowing the man to get beat so that he co uld see how it feels. I advised him that we cou ld not go that route and the pastor forga ve the man. The Pastor said that he is now one of the most fruitful men operating in that region.

He did not know that what he was d oi ng was wrong. It came out through the course of cou nseling that his daddy used to beat his mother. At seven years old this man saw his daddy beat his mother. After beating his mother, his father turned to him and said, "Every woman needs to get beat once in a while, just keep that in the back of your mind." He sa w drinking and he sa w beating. That is why he was born-again yet still drinking and beating his wife. Once he got information and was forgiven, he was delivered. His wife got free and changes started happening. But there mu st be a forgiveness flowin g from the rea lms of those leading us so we can be free in Jesus' name.

Colossia ns 3:13 *"Forbearing one another and forgiving one another if any man ha s a quarrel against any even as Christ forgave you, so also do ye."* If any body has a probl em with you, just as Christ forgave you, likewise forgive them. If you say, "Well, I just have to get to the bottom of the issue," you do not have to get to the bottom of the issue. You just have to forgive them." You know that you cannot find an end to some issues. Stop right there! Father, forgive them.

When they started to stone Steven, his countenance bega n to shine and become gl orified. He sa w the heavens open and Jesus was visible at the right hand of God. What came out of his mouth? "Hold not this sin to their cha rge. Father forgive these people." You know what some of us would have done (as they were stoning us)? "I am not leaving until I take a few of you with me. I curse all of you." You would have started grabbing those rocks and sta rted throw ing those rocks back! Stephen said, *"Hold not this sin to their charge."* It takes a great deal of power to release somebody. The greater person is not the person who is m a king accusations. It is the person releasing.

That is why I love when people come to talk to me. They think that I am not listening. I am listening. But I am n o t going to sit there for two hours listening to all types of foolishn ess. I have never been able to do that. So once I realize that you have ha d troubl e, I will adv ise you to forgive them. I do not know if you realize, but the more you unfold the incident, acids start turning, your face starts cringing, and you begin to go back into the depths of the wickedness. That is why after ten minutes, "I say forgive them." Just release them! In so d oing, you can release yourself. G uess what? Somebody is going to mess up tomorrow so me place, somewhere. So just make up you mind to forgive.